Moments for Moms III Journeys of Joy and Resilience

VISIONARY: Juanita N. Woodson
CO-AUTHORS:

Cystal D. Harrison M.Ed.
Tanisha Graves
Paula Banks
Joi West Phalo
Dani Nicole
Quiniece Noble
Sabrina Clemons
ShaKrystin Jones Dock
Dionne Anderson
Tina Silver

MOMENTS FOR MOMS
VOLUME III
JOURNEYS OF
JOY
&
RESILIENCE

Presented by Grace 4 Purpose, Publishing co.

Moments for Moms III: Journeys of Joy and Resilience

Copyright © 2025 by Juanita N. Woodson,
Cystal D. Harrison M.Ed.
Tanisha Graves
Paula Banks
Joi West Phalo
Dani Nicole
Quiniece Noble
Sabrina Clemons
ShaKrystin Jones Dock
Dionne Anderson
Tina Marie Silver

Published by Grace 4 Purpose, Publishing Co. LLC

All rights reserved. No part of this publication may be reproduced in any form or by any electronic or mechanical means, including information storage and retrieval systems, without prior permission in writing from the publisher, except by reviewers, who may quote brief passages in a review.

All scripture quotations, unless otherwise indicated, are taken from the King James Version of the Bible, unless otherwise indicated. All rights reserved.

ISBN: **979-8-9926893-0-3**

Editing by: Grace 4 Purpose, Publishing Co. LLC

Book cover design by Grace 4 Purpose, Publishing Co. LLC

Printed and bound in the United States of America

DEDICATION

This book is dedicated to every mom who has faced the ups and downs of life with unwavering faith and resilience. To the mothers who have carried the weight of the world on their shoulders yet still find a way to create moments of joy for their families, this is for you.

To the women who have cried silent tears, whispered heartfelt prayers, and pressed on when giving up felt easier, may you see yourself in these pages and know you are never alone.

To the loved ones who support, cheer, and uplift moms in every season, you are the hands and hearts that remind us we are stronger together.

And to you, the reader, may these stories encourage you, inspire you, and remind you that joy is not just a destination but a journey worth embracing every step of the way.

With love and gratitude,
The Authors of *Moments for Moms Volume III*

TABLE OF CONTENTS

Introduction……………………………………………………..2
Chapter One: Paula Banks…………………………………..3
Chapter Two: Crystal D. Harrison……………………….....10
Chapter Three: Dani Nicole…………………………………23
Chapter Four: Tanisha Graves……………………………..30
Chapter Five: Sabrina Clemons…………………………….40
Chapter Six: Joi West Phalo……………………………......48
Chapter Seven: Quiniece Noble…………………………….57
Chapter Eight: ShaKrystin Jones Dock……………………..64
Chapter Nine: Dionne Anderson………………………….....71
Chapter Ten: Tina Marie Silver……………………………..78
Chapter Eleven: Juanita N. Woodson………………………88

Introduction

Motherhood is a journey filled with countless moments—some that make us laugh until we cry and others that strengthen our resolve to keep moving forward. It's in these moments that we discover who we truly are, not just as mothers but as women navigating life's ups and downs.

Moments for Moms III: Journeys of Joy and Resilience is a heartfelt collection of stories written by women who have faced challenges head-on and found joy in unexpected places. Each story is a reminder that, even in the toughest seasons, there is beauty, strength, and purpose waiting to be uncovered.

This book is more than a collection of words—it's a community of voices offering encouragement and connection. Whether you're a mom juggling the chaos of daily life or someone seeking to understand the heart of motherhood, these pages will inspire you to keep going, keep growing, and keep believing in the power of your journey.

Take a moment, breathe deeply, and join us as we celebrate the joy, resilience, and unwavering love that make motherhood so extraordinary.

Moments for Moms III: Journeys of Joy and Resilience

Chapter One
Paula Banks

Growing Together: A Mother's Journey of Resilience and Dreams

"I'm really proud of you, Mom." His words pierced the quiet of the room, settling in the air between us like a gift I had not known I needed. My fingers froze over the keyboard as I slowly turned to face him. My oldest son, no longer the little boy who used to need me at every turn, was now a grown man standing tall in the doorway. He stepped closer and gently rubbed my head which was his signature gesture of affection. He had done this ever since he was little, and in that moment, it was as though time blurred; he was still my baby, even though he now spoke to me as an adult.

I felt something swell in my chest, a mixture of pride, gratitude, and something else I could not quite name. I had not expected this.

For years, I poured my energy into making sure my sons were growing and thriving, often wondering if I was doing enough. Parenting was a constant balancing act being there for every decision, offering advice, and trying to nurture their dreams while quietly pushing mine aside. My husband and I worked together to give them everything they needed, but I often questioned if I could balance motherhood and my own ambitions. Sleepless nights and endless questions filled the years, and somewhere along the way, I convinced myself that motherhood required me to sacrifice my own ambitions.

As they grew older and became more independent, I realized they no longer needed me in the same way. It was then that I knew it was time to pursue the dreams I had set aside—writing. Looking back, I see that it was God's perfect timing. Throughout those years, I had prayed for clarity on how to balance being their mother and still fulfilling my own calling. The answer came in small moments, almost like whispers. Each time I questioned whether I could still follow my dreams, it was faith that reminded me that everything has its season.

My faith carried me through the uncertainty. I learned that trusting in God's timing meant I did not need to rush or control everything; it allowed me to be patient and trust the path unfolding before me. That trust was essential not just in motherhood, but in my own journey toward becoming a writer. I knew I would not have all the answers, but I also knew that God was guiding me through each step, whether I could see the next one or not.

Moments for Moms III: Journeys of Joy and Resilience

Everything I had learned as a mother patience, resourcefulness, and the ability to ask for help became the tools I needed when I took my first steps into self-publishing. It felt as though everything had aligned just when it was meant to.

When my son told me he was proud of me, it was not just a moment of joy it was a culmination of all those moments of letting go. It was the recognition that even as they were growing, I was growing, too. We were navigating this together, both learning what it means to embrace change and trust in the future.

By following my passions, I was showing my sons what it meant to live fully. Through my actions, they learned about resilience and joy, even in moments I did not realize. What I had imparted to them was not one-sided; in their own way, they became my teachers, too. They reminded me that my dreams and my role as a mother were intertwined by pursuing them, I had shown my sons what it means to never give up.

To the mothers reading this: You are more than capable of pursuing your dreams, even if they have been on hold for years. We often tell ourselves that motherhood leaves little room for our own passions, but the truth is, our children learn from how we live, dream, and push forward. They need to see us following our hearts, even when it feels uncertain.

You do not need to wait for the perfect time; sometimes, you just need to take that first step. It is okay to do it scared, without knowing how everything will unfold. The lessons you have learned as a mother; patience, resilience, sacrifice are the same strengths you will draw on as you go after your dreams. You are not just shaping their future; you are shaping your own, and both journeys matter.

Motherhood has taught me how to adapt and grow. Faith has been the foundation of that growth. As Isaiah 41:10 reminds us, *"So do not fear, for I am with you; do not be dismayed, for I am your God. I will strengthen you and help you; I will uphold you with my righteous right hand."* These words have carried me through moments of uncertainty, reminding me that the journey of motherhood is not just about raising them; it is about growing together. It is not just their journey, it is ours.

Paula Banks

Paula Banks is a children's author, creative storyteller, and the founder of EION Books a brand on a mission to celebrate representation and inspire kids to dream big. Through her books and resources, Paula helps kids see themselves in stories, embrace their creativity, and feel empowered to chase their dreams.

With a deep love for hip hop and storytelling, Paula brings bold energy to every project she touches. She's passionate about creating stories that matter—whether she's writing for young readers or helping new authors navigate their journey. Her work reflects her belief that storytelling is a powerful tool to spark confidence, connection, and imagination in every child.

Everything Paula does is rooted in creativity, purpose, and faith. She credits God for guiding her path and blessing her journey every step of the way.

Contact Information:

Social Media: @authorpaulabanks
Website: <u>Eionbooks.com</u>
Email: Contact@paulaybanks.com

Chapter Two
Crystal D. Harrison

Walking Through the Storm with Joy and Resilience

"And we know that in all things God works for the good of those who love him, who have been called according to his purpose". (Romans 8:28)

There are moments in life when joy and sorrow dance together in unity, when resilience is tested to its core, and when we are left wondering how we will keep moving forward in this thing called life. It is in these moments that God's purpose often reveals itself in the most unexpected ways. His presence offers peace, yes even in chaos; His love empowers resilience, even in the darkest of moments. Joy and resilience are not simply emotions we experience; they are spiritual tools that have the propensity to enable us to walk in the fullness of God's purpose for our lives.

July 3, 2020, is forever etched in my mind like it was yesterday. I had been looking forward to a trip back home to Virginia to spend time with my mother, an excitement that quickly faded when the unexpected struck. As I arrived at the hospital where my son, Mekhi, had been rushed after a serious car accident under the train tracks on Morton Avenue in Chester, Pennsylvania the joyful anticipation of family time turned into pure dread.

There, on the hospital stretcher, laid our son, Mekhi, lifeless. The sight was overwhelming. There was so much blood, more than I had ever seen in my life spilled across the floor. Nurses and doctors were swarming around him, their faces concentrated and professional, but beneath that calm exterior, I could feel the intensity of the situation. Tubes were connected to his body, empty blood bags scattered on the floor, and the beeping of machines filled the air. The scene felt surreal, like something out of a war movie. It was utterly terrifying and almost impossible to comprehend.

In that moment, I felt like the world had slowed down, my mind frozen in disbelief. I couldn't make sense of what I was seeing, and I didn't know what to do. Every fiber of my being wanted to scream out for help, for answers, but then, a thought came to me: My husband, Jay would stay calm. He wouldn't panic. He would focus, and begin to intercede on behalf of our son, who lay there, so vulnerable and fragile.

And so, I did what we both knew how to do best, especially in times of crisis: I trusted God. I closed my eyes tight to hold the tears in, but it was too late they were already rolling down my face. I began to pray. I asked God to intervene, to work His Will, and to protect our son. As I prayed, something miraculous happened. I could feel a shift in the atmosphere, something heavy, something dark seemed to lift. The fear, the panic, the sense of impending death began to dissipate. Then I heard the doctor's voice, "We have a pulse. She needs to leave now!"

As I continued to pray, something miraculous began to unfold. Mekhi, who had been unresponsive, slowly started to show signs of life. His color began to return, and the steady beeping of the machines began to sound less ominous. By God's grace, Mekhi pulled through. But it wasn't just a physical healing that took place, it was a spiritual transformation as well.

Though my heart was still broken as I stood there, watching my son in critical condition, a deep peace began to wash over me as I was ushered out of the room. It wasn't the kind of joy that made everything okay, nor did it erase the pain, but it was a peace that transcended understanding, a peace that only God could provide.

In that moment, something unexpected happened. I may not be a great singer, and I've never been one to spontaneously sing in public, but out of nowhere, a song rose within me, "Open the Eye of My Heart, Lord." At first, the words came out quietly, but as I sang, my voice grew stronger, louder, with the conviction that my son needed to hear me. The words became a plea, a prayer for his healing. And as I sang, something miraculous occurred: The noise, the chaos, the panic seemed to melt away. The room began to change even the more. In the midst of all the frantic activity, I could feel His presence, it was so real, so tangible, as if He was right there with me, saying, "I am here, and I am with you.

In the weeks that followed, I found myself reflecting on that moment in the hospital. The joy of peace that filled my heart wasn't a product of the situation changing—it was a product of God's presence in the midst of the storm. His presence didn't make the pain go away, but it gave me the strength to keep going. His love didn't erase the fear, but it gave me the resilience to stand firm, trusting that He was in control.

Resilience doesn't mean you don't feel pain; it doesn't mean you don't cry or feel fear. It means that in the midst of it all, you choose to trust God, knowing that His love and His plan are greater than what you can see with your eyes. That's what I had to do in that moment, I had to choose joy in the midst of sorrow. I had to choose resilience in the face of fear.

Joy and resilience are birthed from a deep-rooted trust in God. It's not a superficial "just smile and everything will be okay" mentality; rather, it's an understanding that even when life feels like it's falling apart, God is still sovereign. He still has a purpose, and He is still at work.

Joy, in its truest form, is not a fleeting emotion dependent on circumstances. It's a fruit of the Spirit that grows in the soil of trust, even in the hardest of times. It's a peace that surpasses understanding, a sense of well-being that transcends human logic. When you are connected to God, you realize that joy isn't just for the good times, it's for the storms too. It's a reminder that God is working, even when we cannot see it.

In the midst of grief, loss, or hardship, God's joy doesn't mean happiness in the traditional sense; it means knowing that He is with us, that He loves us, and that He will never leave us. Even when life seems chaotic, God is still sovereign, still good, and still working out His plan.

Resilience is not about never feeling weak or defeated. It's about having the strength to rise again, to stand firm when everything around you is shaking. It's about trusting in God's promises, even when everything seems uncertain. Resilience is a spiritual muscle that grows as we lean on God's strength instead of our own.

When life knocks you down, resilience doesn't come from gritting your teeth and pushing through on sheer willpower, it comes from surrendering to God and allowing Him to carry you through. It comes from choosing to trust that, no matter what happens, God's purpose is at work in your life.

That day at the hospital, I learned that resilience is birthed in the most painful of moments. It's in those moments where we can either choose to collapse under the weight of sorrow or choose to trust that God is working behind the scenes. And when we choose the latter, joy and resilience will rise within us like a flood.

There are no guarantees in life. We cannot predict the future, and we cannot avoid pain. But we can choose to walk through the storms with God, knowing that He is faithful. Our joy is anchored not in the absence of trials, but in the presence of God in our lives And our resilience comes from trusting that He is using every situation to fulfill His greater purpose.

So, when you face moments of sorrow, fear, or uncertainty, remember this: God is with you. His purpose is at work in your life. His joy is your strength, and His love will empower you to walk in resilience. No matter what comes your way, you can face it with the peace of knowing that He is always with you, always holding you close, and always fulfilling His purpose in your life.

And as for me, I will forever remember that moment in the hospital. It was a reminder that, even in the darkest times, God's joy and resilience are never far from us, He is always near, working in ways we may never fully understand, but always for our good.

Joy is not the absence of suffering or hardship; it is the deep-rooted certainty that God is with us through it all. The Bible speaks of joy as more than just a fleeting feeling, it is a fruit of the Spirit, a characteristic of life lived in Christ. In ***James 1:2*** we are encouraged to ***"count it all joy when you fall into various trials"*** This seems paradoxical, doesn't it? How can we experience joy in the midst of trials? The key lies in the understanding that joy is rooted in something much deeper than the circumstances of our lives.

True joy always comes from knowing God's unwavering presence. It comes from trusting that even in the deepest valleys, He is guiding, protecting, and shaping us. Our joy is not dependent on our situations but on the assurance that God has a plan for our lives, a purpose that far exceeds any temporary pain we may endure. As we embrace God's plan, we begin to realize that joy is not a reaction to what happens around us, but a declaration of faith in what God is doing within us.

The joy that God gives does not disappear when hardship comes; rather, it grows stronger through adversity. It is the quiet confidence that God is working all things for our good **Romans 8:28**. This joy allows us to look beyond the present moment and see a bigger picture, one where God's purpose is being fulfilled, even through our struggles, shortcomings and inward deficiencies.

Resilience is the ability to withstand the challenges of life's hardship and bounce back from each adversity with poise. It is not a trait we are born with, but one that is developed as we walk with God. Resilience is the strength that comes from knowing that God will never leave us nor forsake us **(*Hebrews 13:5*)**. It is the inner fortitude that arises from faith and trust in God's promises.

Consider the life of Apostle Paul. He endured shipwrecks, imprisonments, beatings, and more. Yet, in his letters, he speaks often of rejoicing, of joy in the midst of suffering. In ***2 Corinthians 4:8-9***, Paul writes, ***"We are hard-pressed on every side, yet not crushed; we are perplexed, but not in despair; persecuted, but not forsaken; struck down, but not destroyed***." His resilience was not from his own strength, but from God's strength working in him.

Resilience, like joy, is a divine gift. It comes when we lean on God's power, not our own. When we face trials, our resilience is refined through prayer, Scripture, and a community with fellow believers. It is in these moments that we learn to trust God's timing, to rest in His promises, and to remain steadfast in His love.

The road to resilience is not always easy, but it is always purposeful. God does not waste our suffering; that is what we do when we have solo pity-parties. Every hardship we face is an opportunity for growth, for building endurance, and for developing the character that aligns us with His will. As we grow in resilience, we become living testimonies of God's power at work in us, demonstrating to the world that it is possible to overcome, to thrive, and to rejoice, no matter the circumstance.

Joy and Resilience Builders

1. Root Yourself in God's Promises

James 1:2-3, Psalm 16:11

To walk in joy and resilience, you must first root yourself in God's promises. Joy is not about your circumstances but about your unshakable belief in God's faithfulness. When challenges arise, remember that God's Word holds the key to your joy and strength.

- Set aside time daily for the Word. Meditate on verses that remind you of God's love, His presence, and His promises to never leave you. ***Psalm 16:11*** is a gentle reminder that ***"In Your presence there is fullness of joy."*** This is a joy tha

comes from being close to God, not from external things.
- Memorize and declare God's promises over your life. When you face difficulties, let these truths anchor you and sustain your joy, even in the storm.

2. Embrace Trials as Opportunities for Growth

Romans 5:3-5, James 1:2-4

Resilience is built in the crucible of trials. Rather than viewing hardships as obstacles, choose to see them as opportunities for growth. Every trial has the potential to build your endurance, deepen your faith, and shape you more into the image of Christ. God uses difficulties to refine us, helping us develop the character needed to fulfill His purpose in our lives.

- When facing trials, respond with gratitude and prayer. Instead of asking, "Why me?", ask, "What can I learn from this?" Prayerfully seek God for strength and insight, trusting that He is using the experience for your good *(Romans 8:28)*.
- Celebrate small victories along the way. Acknowledge your progress and resilience in overcoming adversity, and let these moments of growth be a source of joy.

3. Cultivate a Heart of Praise and Gratitude

Scripture Reference: 1 Thessalonians 5:16-18, Philippians 4:4-7

A heart of gratitude and praise has the power to transform your outlook on life. Rejoicing in God, even in difficult times, shifts your focus from the problem to God's power. Gratitude opens the door to joy, while praise brings peace that surpasses understanding. This heart of worship becomes a powerful tool for resilience, reminding you of God's goodness and sovereignty.

- Practice gratitude daily. List things you are thankful for, even in the midst of trials, and acknowledge God's faithfulness in your life. This shifts your perspective and strengthens your resilience daily..
- Develop a habit of praise. Sing, pray, or speak out words of worship, especially when facing challenges. ***Philippians 4:4*** says, "***Rejoice in the Lord always***," a practice that cultivates both joy and resilience in every season.

By walking in these principles daily, you will discover the deep joy and strength that come from relying on God's presence and trusting in His plans for your life.

God's purpose for our lives is both vast and personal. His purpose is to draw us closer to Himself, to shape us into the image of His Son, and to use our lives to bring glory to His name. Every step we take toward that purpose is an act of faith, and in that faith, joy and resilience are essential companions.

When we understand that God's purpose is being worked out in every area of our lives, we can view challenges as opportunities to grow in joy and resilience. Instead of seeing difficulties as obstacles, we can recognize them as steppingstones on the path that leads us closer to God's plan for us.

When we walk in the light of God's purpose, joy and resilience become not only tools for surviving life's hardships but also evidence of the transformative power of His love. Through our joy, the world sees a glimpse of God's goodness; through our resilience, they witness His strength and faithfulness.

To live out joy and resilience requires a daily surrender to God's will. It means acknowledging that we are not in control, but He is. It means choosing to trust in His plan, even when we cannot see the end result. It means cultivating a heart of gratitude, even in the midst of pain, knowing that God is always at work behind the scenes.

To embrace joy and resilience, we must stay rooted in God's Word and in prayer. We must surround ourselves with a community of believers who can support us, encourage us, and pray with us. And we must remember that God's purposes are not always immediately apparent; sometimes, we only see the fruit of our perseverance after time has passed.

But through it all, one truth remains: God's purpose for your life is unshakable, and He is with you every step of the way. Whether in moments of joy or times of trial, He is shaping you, refining you, and preparing you for the good work He has called you to.

And in the end, as we live out His purpose, we discover that true joy and resilience are not merely about enduring life's difficulties but about reflecting His love and power to the world. In our joy and resilience, we become witnesses of God's faithfulness and His never-ending grace.

So, take heart. Keep pressing forward, knowing that the joy of the Lord is your strength *(Nehemiah 8:10)* and that His purpose for you will always lead you to greater peace and fulfillment in Him.

Crystal D. Harrison M.Ed.

Crystal Denise Harrison is a passionate wife, mother, grandmother, community leader, mentor, educator, and pastor. She resides in Chester, Pennsylvania, with her husband of 33 years, Pastor Jay Timothy Harrison Sr., and their family. Together, they pastor True Vine Missionary Full Gospel Baptist Church in Chester, where Crystal serves alongside her husband in ministry. The couple is blessed with eight children—four sons and four daughters—and eight grandchildren.

Crystal accepted Jesus Christ at a young age and has dedicated her life to growing in her purpose for God. She was ordained as a minister in Williamsburg, Virginia, by the late Reverend Edward G. Clemons, and later as an Elder in 2005 by her husband, Overseer Jay Timothy Harrison Sr. She is the founder of **CDH Ministries** and **Heart 2 Heart**, a transformative ministry aimed at empowering women and young ladies of promise. Heart 2 Heart provides a platform for restoring the hearts of women so they can fully experience God's intended purpose for their lives. Through her compassion and dedication, Crystal seeks to guide others on their spiritual journeys.

In addition to her pastoral work, Crystal is an accomplished author and co-author. Her most recent project is *A Bug's Life Alphabet Book*, part of the **Creative Hearts ABC Alphabet Book** series, designed to encourage young children to develop a love for reading and language development. Crystal also co-authored *Faith While Waiting*, a collaboration with her husband and several other notable authors, and her first book, *How to Fight Fair in Marriage*, which provides valuable insights for fostering healthy, lasting marriages.

Crystal is a lifelong educator with over 30 years of experience. She holds a Bachelor's degree in Liberal Arts with a concentration in Early Childhood Education from Hampton University and a Master's degree in Early Childhood Education from the University of Phoenix. Crystal's commitment to children and families is also reflected in her founding of the **Twins Organization**, a tribute to her late sons, Micah and Mekhi.

In her spare time, Crystal enjoys reading, writing, crocheting, and baking. Her favorite children's book is *Leo the Late Bloomer*, a story that highlights the power of purpose in the making. Crystal is also inspired by several Bible verses, including Psalm 22:6, Isaiah 59:19, and Jeremiah 29:11, which have guided her through her journey.

Crystal's unwavering faith, dedication to her family, and passion for helping others have made her an inspirational figure in her community and beyond.

Contact Information:

Email: 4cdhministries@gmail.com
Website: www.CDHMinistries.com
Facebook: Crystal Denise Harrison
Heart 2 Heart
Circle of Educators

Chapter Three
Dani Nicole
A Mother's Pride

Motherhood is important to me because God has chosen the woman to bear the child in her womb. A child is indeed an inheritance, and this role shouldn't be taken lightly. I count it an honor and a blessing to be one of the women God chose to carry three children to full term. Motherhood can be both a challenge and a joyous occasion, my experience with finding joy in the challenging moments comes when I turn small moments into positive moments. Having a spirit of gratitude, connecting with loved ones and pursuing creative outlets helps me maintain a sense of hope during difficult times.

    Before motherhood, I was just your average adolescent woman trying to find her role and purpose in life after graduating high school. I attended college for one year but due to financial circumstances, I decided to go back when I was able to afford to pay for it on my own. So, working a 9-5 was the next step for this college dropout. I also joined a church ministry right after high school and got involved quickly in the choir ministry and children's ministry.

Not long after enjoying my new job and serving in my church, I became pregnant and boy was that a shocker because I was not married and here I was carrying a baby. It seemed like the world had stopped because when the church found out, I was excused from any ministry I was a part of until I had given birth to my child. That hit me hard and even caused me to feel animosity against the church as if the love of God were suddenly sucked out of them because I disobeyed a commandment. I am thankful I had the support of my family, and I knew that God loved me no matter what I had done.

Raising a child was a challenge because this was something for which I had not prepared. I don't think anyone goe into motherhood thinking, well I guess I will just raise this child on my own, at least I didn't. I wanted to do it the right way according to the bible, abstain from sex, wait for the man to find me, court for about a year or two get married, buy the home have the baby and live happily ever after. God had a different plan because that was not at all how it had gone three times. Although my church family had come around and began to support me along with my immediate family the shame and embarrassment stayed with me for a long time because the same thing happened with my second and third children as well.

Like I had mentioned previously, my family has always been a big support for me and my children and now up until today they are supportive and help in any way they can. The state I lived in at time which was Wisconsin had assistance for singled moms such as (WIC) Woman, Infant and Children which provided vouchers for formula, milk, vegetables, and fruit for the child up until the age of five. Childcare assistance was also provided, and food share assistance or SNAP benefits is what they call it now helped with other groceries and medical care through the state was provided.

    I had my children during two stages of my life. I had two children around my early twenties when I was young and felt a little more patient in my life compared to the last child I had when I was in my late thirties which now I think I have lost all my patience. I seemed a little stricter with the older two and a little more lenient with the last child. I tried to instill the same boundaries with both like no dating till sixteen and no late-night game or TV time.

    The challenges I faced with the birth of my children were never a mistake to me. I always found joy because I had always wanted children, I was never set on the number of children, but I knew I wanted children. The husband is coming later and that's ok too. My children are my heartbeat, they are why I go hard so I can leave a legacy they can be proud of. I did the best I could with what I had to provide a safe and protective environment for them. I created memories that we talked about up until today, the movies we watched repetitiously on the VCR and then DVD and the television shows because I could only afford cable in one room of the house so that meant we would be in the living room together.

    Children are an inheritance from God , and I want to be a good steward of what I have inherited (Psalm 127:3) I have learned to establish boundaries that protect them from harm and that teach them to understand that as the parent I must set rules that they need to live by because the world also has rules and there are consequences If rules have been broken. I also learned that an absent father could cause communication barriers, my father was absent many times in my life and that is why although I was a single mom I valued my children spending time with their father over the money. Time is valuable and you can't get time back the way you can get money back.

I also want to conduct myself as a spiritual and moral teacher and I practice this every day with my children even the older they get. I want them to understand that being a parent is a lifelong commitment and that the job is like the 911 operator, 24 hours a day 7 days a week. I also want them to understand that God knows what I am up against, and he will help me when I turn to him in prayer, but praying isn't all I also have work to do.

Always remember, whether you are a single mom, married, divorced, foster, grandmother or acting the role of a mother figure, you can raise a child because God has equipped you to be in that position. He knew this before you were born. (Jeremiah 29:11) He already knows the plans He has for you, so you just have to trust the process and keep the faith. Faith is an action word so that means that you have work to do as well. When you feel discouraged or challenged, call on God in prayer, read scripture, talk to a friend, or turn on a favorite gospel song but get into God's presence whatever that looks like to you. Let that inheritance of motherhood be the greatest joy of your life.

Dani Nicole

Dani Nicole was born in Milwaukee, Wisconsin, and now resides in the thriving city of Charlotte, North Carolina. She is a dedicated mother of three and a hardworking entrepreneur who is not only focused on building her own brand but also on helping others achieve their goals.

Her passion for writing was sparked by her love of reading, which she views as an escape into the lives of characters and the worlds they inhabit. Over the years, Dani has cultivated a deep appreciation for fictional and expressive storytelling, using her creativity to bring her ideas to life on the page.

In March 2024, Dani published her first solo book, *Entangled with Deceit*, a gripping fictional novel that explores the complexities of love intertwined with betrayal and deceit. The story follows Victoria Willis, a character whose journey is filled with joy, excitement, and heartbreak as she searches for love. With its twists and emotional depth, the novel keeps readers on edge, eagerly turning the pages to discover how Victoria's story unfolds.

Dani's writing continues to resonate with readers who appreciate raw, relatable, and emotionally engaging narratives.

Contact Information:

Linktree: https://linktr.ee/dnhall
Website: https://daninicoletheauthor.com/
Facebook: Dani Nicole & daninicoletheauthor
Instagram: daninicoletheauthor

Chapter Four

Tanisha Graves

Delayed but not Denied

"Because your steadfast love is better than life, my lips will praise you"
(Psalm 63:3)

Stereotypes Associated with ADHD

One of the proudest moments of many women is being blessed with the honor to give birth. Not only is it the most rewarding responsibility given to mothers, it is also the most challenging. God gave women the responsibility of carrying a child, feeding and nurturing it from conception until ultimately she dies, or in some instances they die. Most Christian mothers are familiar with God's commands and the high standard He holds parents and children to.

Every mother prays for a healthy child, however in life, we don't always get what we want, instead God gives us what we need. After accepting this particular assignment of contributing my advice to another book honoring the efforts of moms, two scriptures came to mind. One, "Anyone who does not provide for their relatives, and especially for their own household, has denied the faith and is worse than an unbeliever" 1 Timothy 5:8. Two, "For the moment all discipline seems painful who have been trained by it". Hebrews 12:11

As a young and even an immature mother this realization may not occur from the onset, instead it happens after tireless and countless instances of falling on one's face and growing along with the child you are tasked with parenting. By the age of 21, I was a mother of three children. Hmm.. what are most people doing at 21 years old, rejoicing that they can finally drink legally without having to sneak around or camouflage it from older adults. Well I was fostering the futures of three youngsters. Along the way, we endured stigmatism's associated with children with special needs. Not only have I battled and advocated for epilepsy sufferers for the past 32 years but I also dealt with the effects of two other children being diagnosed with Attention-deficit/hyperactivity disorder, better known as ADHD. Over the year, the stigma attached to ADHD has evolved from children being labeled as "problem children" and future menaces to society, to special needs children who are crying out for patience and understanding during their learning and adjustment process. Similar to dyslexia, the person is not "stupid" but possess a unique way of connecting the academic and socialization dots.

My first episode with ADHD began with my firstborn at the tender age of five. There were many days after school when her and I sat at the table going over math problems. We would work the problem out together and when I felt that she had finally gotten it, I left her to herself. I would later return and all her answers were still wrong. My son Marquis was later said to have ADHD also. Both had problems with concentration or one would say retaining the information and hyperactivity.

I would get so upset as we set there for hours on end without a resolution to the problems. I became fatigued and no longer wanted to help complete with the homework assignment and told her to take the work back to the teacher the next morning. The next day after school we were right back at the same drawing board all over again. I was like what is wrong with my child, better yet what is wrong with me? Is it that I don't have what it takes to effectively help my child? Was my answer to give up making my child show no interest? Not only did I have a child with ADHD, I now had another child with Epilepsy, ADHD, and severe mental health issues due to tonic clonic seizures. I felt so defeated!

The struggles had me in meetings and conversations on the phone with my daughter's teachers keeping an update on where she was improving as well as her area of weakness. With my son EIP (Early Intervention Program) meetings were held to set goals to track his progress. One on one help was provided by teachers and after school personnel would help my daughter with her homework assignments and my son had one on one help after school as well to help him until I picked them up.

In those days, teacher often gave mothers of children with behavioral problem what is commonly referred to as the "stank eye". Like, what in the world, did I inherit this school year, or what type of home-training do your child have? These episodes of acting out coupled with a condescending teacher can be demoralizing and can cause the mom to buy into the assumption that she is an unfit mother who allows her child to run around with reckless abandon and no discipline. Teachers famously remember their "good" students, likewise when it comes to students they deemed "bad" they never forget. Then, when another child begins school shortly after the first, the administration begins to assume he or she is guilty by association or that disruption to the class runs in the family. Needless to say, it is not fun for the parent or the child when the latter has established a reputation before they have graduated from grade school.

My daughter Tyrashae may have struggled in school but as she continued with her education she was able to retain and continue on advancing her studies. Today she is a home health nurse, a mother, and has been recognized every quarter as an excellent student and has graduated with her BS in Health Science and throughout has been on National Honor Society for her exemplary grades while being in College. She is also a new upcoming owner of Hearts of Comfort Home Care LLC. Marquis even though he lived his life with epilepsy was an honor roll student and received certificates and acknowledgment from the President Of The USA and legislatures. Marquis lived a life knowing wait he knew taking no as not an answer until he transitioned on home to glory. Maurice who is my other child could have experienced some challenges because of the focus that needed to be given to his sibling but he didn't. Today he is a Top Tier Salesman.

Your child may be delayed but their greater is yet to come. It's not how you start, but how you finish. Pouring into your child and by never giving up, you reap the rewards of the eagerness they develop to further learn and to be of great service to those they were called to serve. You can't give up because that will cause them to walk away or throw in the towel. Instead tell them that they can do all things through Christ that Strengthens them

(Philippians 4:13). Some children will learn quicker than others and that's ok. In my children's struggles they may have been delayed due to ADHD, epilepsy or hyperactivity but they were not denied. Greatness has chased them down and positioned them for greatness.

Seeing my children receiving their education pushed me to go back to school to pursue my GED education. Being to graduating in less than a month. To now in my Doctorate degree in a Bible Counseling in 2025. It is never too late to get your education. It has also encouraged me to have a heart to serve the disability community.

During my journey, I had God who would walk with me and prayer as my weapon for defense. Psalm 121:5 reminds us to not get discouraged because of our present situations but to look to the hill from which comes our help. I knew that my children would be great. God also sent some teachers that were available to help get outside support that helped to improve my children's education.

There were many scriptures and quotes that have helped me to find joy in the journey:

I am who God says that I am. Jeremiah 1:5 states that God knew us even before forming us in our mother's womb. He also stated that He knows the plans for , plans to prosper and not harm us and plans to give us hope and a future. God is saying I am here to elevate you to your greater. For your greater is in your later.

If I cannot do great things, I can do small things in a great way."
—Martin Luther King Jr.

Defeat is not the worst of failures, not to have tried is the true failure.

— George Edward Woodberry

We may encounter many defeats, but we must not be defeated. It may even be necessary to encounter the defeat, so that we can know who we are.
— Maya Angelou

Remember these practical tips:

1. Education is key
2. Perseverance is necessary
3. Embrace the joys that come with parenting
4. Be thankful in All Things

My Babies! My heart flips overtime because of who you are and what you mean to me! Marquis we miss you down here but God had other plans for you.

Tyrashae   Marquis (my angel)   Maurice

Tanisha Tyler Graves

Tanisha Tyler Graves is the author of "I Pulled the Sun out for You", and Co – Author in two Amazon Best Seller books– *Moments for Moms Vol II"*, and *Faith While Waitin*g. Minister Graves has been recognized in 2023 as Community Leader of the Year by Power and Grace Leaders, in 2024 Community Leader of the Year by Family Bash and most recently in 2024 as Non-Profit of the Year by Designed for A Purpose. She is a minister, wife, mother, and grandmother who has a great love for God, family, and the well-being of others. The love she shares for others was intensified after the loss of her first-born son who passed away suddenly on September 2, 2019. During bereavement, she contemplated giving up, but God had other plans, explaining, "I'm going to use you, my child, for My Glory." Minister Graves now spends her time pouring and encouraging others as an Evangelist giving testimonies about what the Lord has done for her and what He is capable of doing for them as well.

She faithfully serves her local communities and abroad, speaking on behalf of the voiceless, their families, and those impacted by health disparities. In addition, she assists the government with investigating and researching ways to improve the quality of life of those suffering from Seizure-related brain trauma. This fall, Minister Graves will be furthering her ministerial calling by enrolling in the Williamsburg Theological Seminary Doctorate program in Biblical Counseling and graduating in 2025.

Contact Information:

Website: TanishaTylerGraves.com
Wtts4epilepsy.org
Operationloveinc.org
Facebook: Tanisha Graves

Chapter Five

Sabrina Clemons

Clouds and Rainbows
"Joy does not simply happen to us. We have to choose joy every day."
~ Henri Nouwen

In this journey called life, we all experience cloudy days, often looking for the sun to shine again. Sometimes those cloudy days get so dark it seems like we will never see the light.

However, the truth is there is always light behind the darkness and somewhere over the clouds there is a rainbow. The question is how do we find joy in the days that get so cloudy? Is joy really a choice? If we pause and think about this, the answer is yes, joy is a choice. It is not always an easy choice, yet it is something that we have to be intentional about choosing daily.

I have found the mom journey to be a beautiful journey. It is not always easy, sunny or come with roses. However, it is still rewarding. Daily we are giving and sacrificing, most likely putting ourselves last. We are usually considering the needs of our children first, as we should because let's face it, they didn't ask to be here. However, they are here and we have a responsibility to love, nurture, and care for them. In return, they love us back. We can find joy by embracing this.

Cloudy Days

"MOM, I need you" "MOMMY, please help me!" These are the cries we often here from our children regardless of age. They may sometimes not consider that in the midst of their needs, that you sometimes have needs too. A need to find your happy place, stay there and enjoy it a little bit. A need for moments of peace. We sometimes go through personal trials and tribulations that they know nothing about because we choose to protect them and cover our anguish, heartaches, and pains with a smile. However, sometimes children are more vigilant and aware then we think, and they see and feel what we go through. Our cloudy days can become their cloudy days and vice versa. Truthfully speaking, it can be hard to find joy in those days, and as a mom it can be hurtful.

Moms face challenges. It's inevitable. I've experienced some really dark and cloudy days too. I remember going through a valley experience in my marriage and this experience put me into a deep depression. Depression had such a grip on me to the point I couldn't get out of bed, and I would lay for days, curtains pulled and in the dark under the covers. I didn't want to eat nor see or talk to anyone. My children were younger at this time. They were at an age where they needed their momma, and I knew this. However, the pain was so deep, I could not see through the tears. So many days and nights I cried and really wanted to scream, but couldn't because I wanted to protect them. However, my little ones knew that something was wrong. They knew I wasn't myself and in their minds I'm sure they didn't really know what to do. I felt like during this season I checked out on them, yet they still needed me and in spite of, they loved me through it all. I didn't, well really couldn't at the time, consider how my trauma and depression would affect them in the present or in their future. However, it very much so did. They did not always see me making the healthiest choices to deal with depression. Believe it or not our choices and what we model definitely influences our children's choices and actions. Sometimes this can affect how they develop as well as their moods and mental health. So later in their adolescent and teen years, they didn't always make the best choices and I could see how my seasons of depression affected them. I carried the guilt of not only allowing depression to consume me to the point of depriving time with my children, but also see how the broken pieces later affected them. There wasn't any joy nor any rainbows in sight in that season!

Joy in Resilience

"Girl get up, you got this!" I really tried to tell myself this on those cloudy days, but it was not that easy. Can you relate? I was not happy and I lost my joy for a season. The only glimpse of sunshine were my children. Although they never said anything, they knew joy was not in the air in our household. I sensed their sadness through their smiles. Nevertheless, they would still come with their love, hugs, and kisses. Children are the most resilient little beings on this earth Although they may experience challenges, family trauma or sadness, they learn to bounce back. It doesn't mean they never are upset or think negatively but they do learn how to find positivity in the negativity. Your child is the one who will look you in the face and tell you it's going to be okay. There is always tomorrow and with that you are given a new day with a fresh start.

Joy in the Morning

That is actually the good news. Trouble don't last always and it really will be okay. Psalms 30:5 (KJV) says "Weeping may endure for a night, but a shout of joy comes in the morning." This verse is a reminder that even though we may experience sadness, trauma, or sorrow, joy will come. We have to believe that. Joy really does come in the morning. Sometimes you have to make a decision and embrace the truth of God's word and just get up, maybe even shout! That coupled with the love of God and your children is a sure formula for your joy to be restored and add to your ability to bounce back. I had to make a decision to intentionally get up and get my joy back and I did just that. The love of my children impacted my resiliency greatly. I embraced their love, and was reminded to have gratitude concerning them. Our children are gifts and actually add joy to our lives. Because of God's love, I was able to forgive myself and let go of the weight of guilt and shame concerning depression.

Enjoy watching the rainbow

After rain and storms, sometimes a rainbow appears. When facing those cloudy days, you have to challenge yourself to choose joy in spite of. I get joy when I see rainbows because they always remind of God's promises. His promises are truth, and they speak life to your heart and spirit. Finding joy in His promises will help you to bounce back. Other practices that will help you to maintain your joy in resiliency are through prayer, asking God to restore your joy, focusing on the little things that bring joy, and be grateful about it. In spite of
any challenges that you may face, always remember that joy will come in the morning.

Additionally, let the joy of the Lord be your strength. Making that choice will help you see past the clouds and see the beauty of the rainbow.

I leave you with a couple of scriptures to meditate on. Write them on the tablet of your heart. May you be strengthened by them, His Word, His presence and your joy remains;

"May the God of hope fill you with all joy and peace in believing, so that by the power of the Holy Spirit you may abound in hope."
(Romans 15:13)

"You make known to me the path of life; in your presence there is fullness of joy; at your right hand are pleasures forevermore."
(Psalm 16:11)

Sabrina L. Clemons

Sabrina L. Clemons is a kingdom-minded woman of faith with a kingdom assignment. Her purpose is to be about her Father's business bringing glory to Him in everything she does, while speaking truth in love, life and healing, and the oracles in which the Father reveals and chooses her to speak. Ordained and consecrated in 2006, she has led different teams in ministry over the years to include Women's Ministry, Christian Education, Intercessory Prayer, and Children's Church. She has served as a Church Administrator, and in the role of Co-Pastor while her husband led Resurrection House International Ministries.

Currently, her assignment in marketplace ministry is serving and leading as a regional director for a nonprofit organization and she is the founder of a budding ministry - Rising From the Ashes. She is dedicated to providing services that stimulates and enhances growth, development, and solutions for mind, soul and spirit, while advancing the kingdom agenda.

Sabrina L. Clemons is a graduate of Norfolk State University and continued her graduate studies at Hampton University. Additionally, she continued her ministry studies through the Freedom (Life) School of Ministry, and currently through Eagles International Training Institute. She is a contributing author in the books 'Hear Me Roar' and 'The Traits of Women of Grace' and Moments For Moms Volume II.

Sabrina feels especially called to the family mountain – women and children, particularly those who have experienced trauma, more specifically domestic & sexual violence. She coaches and mentor youth and young adults that have been victimized and/or experienced trauma in their lives. Being a survivor of such experiences, she easily identifies and empathize with all who has experience such.

Her faith in God has empowered her to be resilient. She is determined to help others experience resurrection power, restoration, and freedom through what she offers in business and ministry. In addition to being an administrator, Sabrina is an educator and advocate that works within her community. She serves on several collaborative teams, taskforces and coalitions. She is the proud wife of Elder Anthony Clemons and the mother of two beautiful, gifted daughters – Rachel and Sarah.

Contact the Author:
Email: thekingsagenda12@gmail.com
Social Media: http://linktr.ee/sabrinacspeaks
Website: www.sabrinalclemons.com

Chapter Six

Joi West Phalo

If I Got Through It, You Can Too….

Defying the odds and exceeding societies expectations is what I did. Achieving goals, such as: graduating from high school to obtaining a bachelor's degree in Human Resources and building a better life for myself and my son. Through hard work, determination, and a made-up mind and most importantly through resilience; I made it! We made it!

At 14 years old, I became pregnant, at the age of 15 I gave birth to a baby boy and named him Jayden. I had no idea that could even happen to me at such a young age. I mean, I knew what I was doing -- skipping school and having sex. I just didn't think I would actually get caught. But hey, I did. I had to learn how to adapt to a life I never envisioned for myself and chose not to let becoming a teen mom determine the total outcome of my life. Even though the challenges were hard, I remained resilient and found joy in some of the tough times. In this chapter I will give you a glimpse into my journey of becoming a teen mother, and how I chose to not let it determine the total outcome of my life, even though the challenges were hard.

At that time, I thought my life was over. My goal was to finish high school so that I could go to college to create a better life for myself and my baby. I was so determined not to be a statistic, and my parents made sure that I wasn't. I can't lie at times, I wanted to give up, but I couldn't. I knew I wanted more for me and my baby. I had to grow up a lot faster than the average teenaged girl, and I didn't get to experience prom, parties, or sleepovers. You know, things I should have been enjoying at that age. The reality is that there were lots of things I wanted to do but couldn't, because I had a baby to tend to. It wasn't a baby doll that I could just toss aside when I wanted to do something more fun. This was my actual baby…a living, breathing, real baby that depended on me -still a child- for everything. At times, it was very depressing, but I had to snap out of it really quick. Don't get me wrong, if it was something I wanted to do sometimes, my mom would babysit. It wasn't often that I went places with friends, though. My life had become so different, so fast.

Fast forward a little, When I was 19 years old and Jayden was around four, I got married. I know, I was super young. As you can tell, I've done a lot of things at a young age. I felt like I was ready to be on my own and Jayden's dad felt the same way. I guess you can say I was ready to be grown, as the old folks say. So, he and I talked things over and decided, *You know what? Let's do it*. This was not the way I wanted to get married. I'd always dreamed of a surprise proposal with a fairytale wedding to follow. None of that happened. Instead, we went to the courthouse. It was easy, simple, and quick. It was so quick; it really didn't seem like we were married for real.

We took the weekend and moved in our first little apartment as a family. It was an adjustment for both of us. We settled into our married life, doing the best we knew with the level of knowledge and maturity we had. After two years of marriage, I became pregnant, but I miscarried. I wasn't sad. Truthfully, it was a relief; we were not ready for another baby at that time. Shortly after, though, I was pregnant again. Everything went great with the pregnancy, and I gave birth to a baby girl named Jayla on March 4, 2008. Having two children and being a young married couple had its challenges. As much as I wanted us to do things together, we didn't. We never had date night with just the two of us. Sometimes, we would have company over and play cards or something. For the most part, though, we really didn't have alone time. We would go to his parents' house on Sundays, but we drove separate cars, and whenever I went to my dad's for family functions, he wouldn't go. My marriage was nothing like I envisioned, but we kept going through the motions.

A few years later, I was pregnant again. This time it was kind of a surprise. I say that because I was in-between birth control at the time of conception. We were not in a good space as husband and wife because he was doing whatever he wanted to do. You know, being married is a huge sacrifice, because there are certain things you can't do, or at least you shouldn't. Sometimes, you have to change your circle, and definitely change your mindset. I definitely think that was too big of an adjustment for him. We ended up separating when I was five months pregnant with baby number three. He moved back with his parents, and I moved back with my mom and stepdad. Yep, my pregnant self and two kids moved back home. It wasn't that bad, because I knew I wouldn't be alone with the kids, and I would have help. It was still an adjustment, however, considering my mom's house was not kid-friendly, and I was used to my own space. But it all worked out.

On October 7th, 2010, our second son and third child, Jaxon, was born. When I returned home after giving birth to Jaxon, I was determined to find a good job and move out of my mom's house. I was laser-focused on re-establishing my life as a single mom of three.

A few months passed, and he was trying to get back with me. but after how he left me and the kids, I was not hearing it at all. And at this time, he had a baby on the way with someone else, even though we were still legally married. I couldn't allow myself to go back to him. I knew nothing would be different, so my mind was made up that I wanted a divorced and was going to get myself together for my three children. As the song says, *When a women's fed up/There ain't nothing you can do about it.* I was fed up. I filed for a divorced, and it was a bittersweet day for me. I couldn't believe I was 23 years old with 3 children and divorced. Some days it would wear me down mentally but, for the most part, I was strong. My biggest disappointment was being a single mother. At times, all I could think about was that I was a 23-year-old grown woman living with my parents with my three children. I couldn't understand why my life was going this way; I created a plan and set some goals to achieve them. I did not want to live with my parents forever, so I knew I had to make some things happen to change that. In 2009, I got a Bachelor's Degree in Human Resource and I never found a job in that field, so I decided to go back to school to get an alternative master's in education. Becoming a teacher wasn't necessarily what I wanted to do, but considered my children and how it would be a good career choice that wouldn't keep me away from them too much. I needed something flexible, and school hours are perfect. The kids and I would basically have the same schedule -- off at the same time for holidays, spring and summer breaks, and I'd be off work at the same time they got out of school. That way, I wouldn't have to really worry about a sitter. In-between pursuing my degree, I become a paraprofessional. That's just a long name for a teacher's aide. I was able to take my older kids with me, and Jaxon went to daycare.

About a year later I found a house to rent. I was so excited because it was right on time. The kids and I could finally have our own place. As I sit back and reflect over those years, I have no idea how I did it alone with 3 kids. It was literally just me and my children. A year and a half after settling into my single life, I thought I was ready to date again. Truth was I wasn't, I was in three relationships after divorcing and one was a domestic violence situation and he hit me one time and I knew then that I wasn't going to put up with that. After that failed relationship, I was tired. I had finally decided that I would find *Joi* and get to know who I really was. What I mean by finding out who Joi really was. I mean getting to know my worth, my wants, and my needs. I also, had to distant myself from negative people, because being around negative would drain me. So once I started hanging around positive people I noticed, I would be happier, I would speak positive words over my life and my kids' life and our days would be better.

Once I started feeling better about the new Joi that I was becoming; I would pray for the kind of guy that I wanted in my life; because I knew I didn't want to be single all my life. I was still young and I wanted to be married, but I knew I needed God's help this time, because I was failing trying to do things on my own. I remember praying to God for a man that would love me for me, and love my kids like they were his own. I knew whoever this man was, he had to be sent by God. Well, just a few weeks later, I meet this guy named Derrick. On May 29th, 2014, was another day that changed my life. We got married. This was my second marriage, and I promised myself it would be my last. Together, we made a vow that we would make our marriage lasting and happy. We aren't perfect, and we've had our challenges as a blended family, but we are still going strong today by the grace of God.

Although my life didn't turn out the way that I envisioned it but Such is life, right? It was nowhere in my vision that I'd become a mother at 15, married at 19, and divorced at 23, but that is exactly where my choices landed me. To some, this may sound like a sad, unfortunate story. For me, it's not that at all. It's the life I unexpectedly experienced, but it is also the experiences that developed me. Was it ideal to become pregnant at 14? Absolutely not; however, it is a reality that so many girls face in today's world. These life experiences changed me as a person I shifted my mindset, my view on understanding others' struggles has increased, my prioritization skill has become impeccable, I've become more resourceful My faith has strengthened. As a mother these experiences helped me release fear, awakened my sense of empathy, realized my purposes in life it's more than being a mother, I have a new sense of motivation. Don't be hard on yourself in learning the ropes as a new mother, you won't be perfect. Just stay focused on being the best mother you can be to your child. Your presence is far better than any gift you could ever give them.

Joi West Phalo

Joi West Phalo is the author of four current published works, most recently, *She Changes Everything: The Wheel of Life Workbook*. She is the founder of She Changes Everything, an organization created to inspire and encourage teen moms and teen girls to overcome the shame, adversities, stereotypes, and challenges of young motherhood through community, education, resources, and literature. She is also one of the co-founders of H.O.P.E Podcast (Helping Organize Postive Parenting Effectively), a new podcast focused on empowering and supporting teem moms and young adults.

An inspirational quote from her novel 15.19.23. recently made an appearance on the Jennifer Hudson show in the form of a featured coffee mug moment! She was selected as a Distinguished Author of Alabama by the Better Together Book Tour for the month of June in 2023. She was also chosen as one of the Inspiring Women of the Gulf Coast in 2024.

She obtained a Bachelor of Science in Human Resources Management from Faulkner University. For eight years, Joi worked with the Mobile County Public School System as a Paraprofessional and Registrar; For four years Joi served as an administrative coordinator for the Center For Fair Housing. She is currently an associate personal banker for Wells Fargo.

In her debut novel, *15. 19. 23.*, she details her experiences with teen pregnancy and motherhood, young marriage, and divorce. Phalo prioritizes community impact and keeps invoking positive change at the heart of her work. Her ultimate goal is to change lives one book at a time! When she is not cultivating her purpose and passions, Joi enjoys cooking, traveling, and spending time with family.

She is a devoted wife to her husband Derrick and mother to their four children.

Contact Information:

Website: Www.joiwestphalo.com
Email: Shechanges1@gmail.com
Facebook: Joi West Phalo/ She Changes Everything

Chapter Seven
Quiniece Noble
Motherhood Meets Resilience

"They say motherhood changes you, but I never understood how much until I held my child for the first time in July 2016"

They say motherhood changes you, but nothing prepared me for just how much it would shape me, stretch me, and redefine everything I thought I knew about myself.

Motherhood is a journey full of unexpected twists and turns, moments of pure joy, and some of the hardest challenges I've ever faced. Through my journey as a mother, I found resilience in the chaos, strength in the struggle, and love in the most unexpected places.

Before I became a mother, my life was one of balance—or so I thought. By day, I worked as a preschool teacher, pouring my heart into the little ones I cared for. By night, I let loose in the nightlife, chasing the freedom that came with it. I didn't see any reason why I couldn't keep living like that. Life seemed steady enough.

Then Maurice came along, and everything shifted. We weren't strangers, but it had been years since we last crossed paths. What started as a casual conversation quickly turned into something more. Before I knew it, we were wrapped up in each other, and six weeks later, I found out I was pregnant.

Maurice already had four kids, but he was excited to have another I, on the other hand, felt a mix of emotions—mostly fear. I had no idea what motherhood would look like for me, but I was determined to figure it out.

When Maurice and I moved in together to prepare for the baby, I thought we were building something stable. But life had other plans. Just weeks before I gave birth, Maurice went to jail, leaving me alone to navigate the final stretch of my pregnancy.

Montana's birth was one of the happiest days of my life, but it was bittersweet. Maurice wasn't there, and I felt the weight of doing it all alone.

At first, I didn't know how I was going to manage. There were days when I felt like I couldn't do it, but every time I looked at Montana, I found the strength to keep going. My family and friends stepped in to help, reminding me that I didn't have to do everything on my own.

When Maurice came home two years later, things weren't perfect, but we were hopeful. He had his struggles, especially with addiction, and that brought a lot of tension into our home. I tried to hold everything together for Montana, for myself, and for Maurice, but the chaos eventually became too much.

Walking away from Maurice wasn't easy. I didn't want to give up on him, but I knew Montana deserved stability and peace. Even after we separated, I stayed by his side, offering support in the ways I could, because I still cared about him deeply.

In the middle of the struggle, there were moments that reminded me of why it was all worth it. Like the first time Montana called me "Mama," or when he took his first steps and I realized just how quickly he was growing up.

One Christmas, Maurice was home, and Montana was so excited to wake up and see him there. That holiday felt like a glimpse of the family we wanted to be. Even though things didn't turn out the way I hoped, those moments of joy were enough to keep me going.

Looking back, I see how much this journey has shaped me. I've learned that resilience isn't about being unbreakable; it's about letting yourself bend, heal, and grow. Montana gave me a reason to keep fighting, and I'm stronger because of it.

To the moms out there who feel like they're drowning: You're not alone. You're doing better than you think, and your children see your effort, even when it feels like no one else does. Lean on the people who love you, and don't be afraid to ask for help.

Motherhood has been the hardest and most beautiful thing I've ever done. It's taught me how to love deeply, fight fiercely, and find joy in the small things.

Whatever your journey looks like, know that it's okay to stumble. It's okay to fall apart sometimes. What matters is that you keep showing up—for your kids, for yourself, and for the life you're building.

God is within her, she will not fall; God will help her at break of day." – Psalm 46:5

Resources for parents:

Office of head start https://eclkc.ohs.acf.hhs.gov/

Urban League : https://nul.org/

Department of children and family services: https://dcfs.louisiana.gov/

Planned Parenthood: https://www.plannedparenthoodaction.org/

Jobs https://job1nola.org/

Medicaid: https://ldh.la.gov/subhome/1

WIC: https://www.wichealth.org/

https://www.asaniheartbeat.org/

Quiniece Noble

Hi Moms! "Greetings from New Orleans, where culture, resilience, and celebration come alive!"

Quiniece Noble is a proud New Orleans native, a devoted mother, and the author of six impactful books. With a background in early childhood education and experience as a parent leader, Quiniece brings a wealth of knowledge and a deep passion for empowering others.

Her commitment to her community shines through her work as a youth mentor, where she dedicates her time to uplifting young girls in the Greater New Orleans area through mentorship programs and summer youth initiatives. Quiniece is also a creator of meaningful children's books, self-help journals, and other resources designed to inspire growth, resilience, and self-discovery.

Quiniece's dedication to giving back is evident in her ability to connect with both children and adults, sharing her personal experiences and professional expertise to encourage others to embrace resilience in their own lives. She has a special heart for single mothers, providing them with encouragement and tools to navigate the challenges of motherhood.

Whether she's mentoring, teaching, or reading to children, Quiniece Noble is making a lasting impact by celebrating the strength, culture, and spirit of New Orleans while empowering others to rise to their full potential.

Contact Information:

Instagram: nee_thenobleone
Facebook: Quiniece Noble

Email: authorquiniecenoble@gmail.com

Chapter Eight

ShaKrystin Jones-Dock

Surviving Placenta Previa

"I don't look like what I've been through." This is my favorite quote because it describes my life. The joy of becoming pregnant when you are married is something that a lot of women hope for. We often do not know some of the challenges we may face throughout our pregnancy journey. For me, I learned about the pregnancy complication called placenta previa. There are so many complications and experiences that we do not know about or what you can do when faced with those complications because they are not discussed.

As a mother of three now, for ten years I thought my first child, DJ, would have been my only child. Constantly visiting my OBGYN, and trying to figure out my options to conceive, I was told I had endometriosis, and I would not be able to have any more kids. As a woman that information did not sit well with me, so in 2018 I changed doctors. The new OBGYN told me to give my body six months to a year to make sure that there was no birth control in my body. Soon after, the world shut down because of Covid-19, and a year later I found out I was pregnant in July 2020 with my second child Dash. He was born in January 2021. Fast forward a year later, I found out I was pregnant again with my third child in January 2022; that was a surprise. Now I have gone from having one child for ten years to now my husband and I are about to be a family of five.

The time is now April 2022 and my husband, Dion, and I are heading to the doctor's appointment to find out the gender of the baby. Emotions were high because it was going to be a surprise because we were having a gender reveal this weekend. After seeing the ultrasound technician, we went in to see my doctor. The doctor came in and he was very blunt. He told my husband and I that during the ultrasound scan, the tech discovered that I had placenta previa. Of course, I have no idea what this is, so I asked if he could explain. As defined by the Mayo Clinic (www.mayoclinic.org) placenta previa is a problem during pregnancy when the placenta completely or partially covers the opening of the uterus(cervix). The placenta is an organ that develops inside the uterus during pregnancy, to give oxygen and nutrition to the baby and to remove waste. The placenta connects to your baby through the umbilical cord. Normally, the placenta is attached to the top side of the inner wall of the uterus. This can cause a portion of the placental tissue to cover the cervix and can result in bleeding during the pregnancy or after the delivery. Changes in the uterus and placenta can lead to the problem correcting itself. If it doesn't the baby will have to be delivered by cesarean section (C-section).

After receiving this information, I felt hurt, upset, and less than motherly. The doctor told me not to stress, and that the main symptom of placenta previa would be bleeding that occurs after

20 weeks (about 4 and a half months) of pregnancy. I was nineteen weeks, and I had no sign, so I knew I had to take it easy. I had two appointments in May. The doctor's visit was good; good vitals and no bleeding. With my baby due in September, I was hopeful that this condition would correct itself. As I prepared for the closing of the school year at my job, I knew summer break was near and that I could get all the rest I needed to help me prepare for the baby, but boy was I wrong.

On May 31, while at work I felt an unusual feeling, so I stepped in the restroom and just as I figured— bright red blood flowing out. I came out and immediately called my doctor's office. They told me to get there as fast as I could. When I arrived at the OBGYN office and was seen, I was immediately sent to the emergency room. This first emergency hospital visit was not my last.

When I arrived at the ER and signed in, I was immediately put in a labor and delivery room and got hooked up on the monitor. The first overnight stay was hard on me because I was not sure what to expect. Is my baby, okay? Was I about to deliver early? After the second day in the labor and delivery ward, the bleeding had slowed down, it was spotty, so I was moved to a regular room. My vulnerability kicked in because I am missing my home life. Now, everything is falling on my husband. I still have DJ and Dash at home–a one year old baby and a ten-year-old who relies on their mom. And being that it is post Covid, the hospital has a restriction on any visitors under 18, so this means I could not even see my kids. At this time, I started begging the doctor to let me go home, but I was told that I could go downstairs to see them for no more than an hour. After a week in the hospital, the bleeding finally stopped, but my placenta was lining the bottom of my uterus, so I was released to go home, but I was put on bedrest. After two more emergency room stays throughout June and July, the doctor informed me that if I were rushed back to the ER, I would have to stay there until my baby was due in September. I was not staying in the hospital for 2 months, so I made sure that I followed the doctor's orders.

As summer was ending and school was starting back, I was home to see my 6th grader off to middle school and 2-year-old to daycare before my doctor's appointment. Today, I am 33 weeks (about 7 and a half months), and I was getting an ultrasound. As soon as the tech examined me the blood began flowing. So, the doctor told my husband and I that I should head to the hospital, just so they could monitor me. I declined that instantly because I knew that would lead to me staying in the hospital for 6 weeks (about 1 and a half months). I told them I was going home and monitor the bleeding and if it worsened then I would return to the hospital.

Later that evening, we ate dinner, and my oldest son said, "Mom let us take some pictures of us before Drue arrives. "As my husband, Dion, gets his phone out, we all gathered on the sofa making silly faces. DJ, Dash, and I took a few pictures in front of the TV. Dion yells "Ok, one more family of four picture before we become a family of five. After the family photo shoot, it was time to get the boys ready for bed.

As I was getting ready for bed, I went to use the restroom and my water broke, along with the biggest blood clot I had ever seen. Dion called his parents to get the kids, and we rushed to the hospital. As I was rushed into the delivery room to get my epidural, they made my husband wait as they prepared me; 10 minutes later at 9:34 pm on August 10, 2022, my baby Drue was born. This was such a joyous moment! Even though I was completely unaware of anything that had occurred in the last 10 hours, as I woke up, I could tell it was drastic because I was in tons of pain. With my husband by my side checking to see if I was okay, I asked him where my baby was. He was in the NICU because he was premature, and I could see him once I got up. The doctor came in to see how I was feeling. He told me he did a tubal ligation procedure on me after delivering the baby. I asked if that was why I was in so much pain, he explained that if the pain did not ease up by noon, that he would have to take me in for an emergency hysterectomy. Once, he turned around at 11:30 am, the doctor told me I was going downstairs for the procedure. Dion and I were so nervous and knew this was a lot on my body after just delivering my baby last night. After the hysterectomy was complete and I was back in my room, I was finally able to see my precious baby boy. The moment when I held him was so emotional, knowing the journey I just went through to have him and make sure that he was healthy is beyond words, and I was so grateful to God for making sure my health and my body was strong enough to birth this beautiful creation.

After experiencing placenta previa and knowing the severity of it, I take my health very seriously. As mothers, we tend to put our family's needs before ours, but if something happens to us, who is going to take care of the family? If at any time something feels wrong concerning your health, and this is for anyone, not just a pregnant woman, contact your physician or call 911.

Always follow your heart! I knew more children were in my future and I did not let one doctor stop me. Since this experience, I have sought medical advice from another doctor and in the end, I had two more babies. The last one took me on this journey from being in and out the hospital, major bleeding, arriving early, tubes tied, and hysterectomy. When I quote "I Don't Look Like What I've Been Through" I mean that. This is a true testimony to me SURVIVING PLACENTA PREVIA!

ShaKrystin Jones-Dock

ShaKrystin Jones Dock is a dedicated wife and mother of three from Mobile, Alabama. As the author of *Surviving Placenta Previa*, she shares an emotional and inspiring account of her personal pregnancy journey while navigating the challenges of this rare and unexpected condition. Through her writing, ShaKrystin seeks to empower pregnant women to trust their bodies, advocate for their health, and confidently raise their voices to ensure the well-being of both themselves and their babies.

Contact information:

Facebook: ShaKrystin Jones Dock
Instagram: author_shajdock
Email: shakrystindock@gmail.com

Chapter Nine
Dionne Anderson

Authentically Me

William Shakespeare said, "To Thy Own Self Be True". What Do You Want?? Someone asked me this question a couple of months ago and I realized I never really thought about me. I have gone through this journey being a mom to my little sisters after my mother died of breast cancer when I was 15 and my siblings were 16, 7 and 5 years old. I am grateful my grandparents chose to keep us together and raise us when they were at a place in life where they had raised all their children and now were going to start over with me and my siblings.

When I was in my senior year of high school and getting ready to graduate with a scholarship to Western Michigan University, I found out I was pregnant with my son Trevor. I was scared to tell my grandparents because I was from a very religious family and for them to find out I had been having sex outside of marriage was a huge no-no. That summer I went away to college and did not tell anyone except my best friend about my pregnancy. No one knew right away but there were signs, and I tried to hide it from everyone. Since I was overweight, it was easier to hide it by wearing baggy clothes. I went to the university health clinic once but never returned for any prenatal care. All of a sudden I started having freak accidents where I would fall and land directly on my stomach. I would get out of the bed and slip on a non-skid rug, I would walk up the steps, trip and land on my stomach. I remember the last fall like it was yesterday, I was walking down a hill on campus and the next thing I know I was rolling down the hill and landed right on stomach. One of my friends laughed and said, "girl we thought you were never going to stop rolling". I got up and laughed it off saying I was just clumsy but inside I knew that these incidents were not accidents and I was carrying a gift that was going to be great one day and I was going to do everything in my power to make sure to keep my baby.

Fast forward 15 years, my son Trevor is a high school sophomore on his way to becoming a highly sought after football star. I put my life on hold to help raise my son, sisters, and my nieces and nephews. I was also working to build my career. Rarely did I put myself first. My life was church, family and work for years.

During this time I started traveling for my job and was in a hotel one morning looking in the mirror and noticed a lump on my right breast. Since my mom passed from breast cancer, I would make it a point to get a mammogram every year. The year before my doctor found a cyst in my left breast but it was found to be benign and an aspiration was done, and I was good to go. This time it was different, I noticed it was sore, red and felt about the size of a small golf ball. I made a mental note to call my doctor when I got back home. Well life goes on and it was a couple of weeks before I called the doctor and made an appointment. The doctor examined me and did a mammogram the same day. While I waited for the results, a nurse came in and said she needed to do an ultrasound. While she doing the ultrasound, I looked at the screen and saw this dark mass. I asked her what it was, and she avoided answering. Later the doctor came in the room and said they were going to run some blood tests and they would call me with the results. I went home and three days later, the doctor called and wanted to set up an appointment for me to come back in for the results. I thought this was odd, so I asked a friend to come with me.

"You have cancer"
To hear those words shook me but in that very moment I heard a still voice say, "but it's not unto death". I was a single mom and all these years it has been me and my son. I was determined to live, I did not want anyone else raising my son! I had a double mastectomy but was not able to do reconstruction due to my size. I remember my first chemo treatment, some of the side effects and thought well maybe I'll lose weight. Well guess what, one of the side effects of my chemo was weight gain! I just sat there and had a good laugh. I feel going through the treatment, the surgery, people's misconception about cancer and just fear that I might die scared my family. I could see it in their eyes when they would look at me. I felt they thought I would die like my mother did. So, I did not tell them much about what I was feeling or experiencing, I just kept it bottled up on the inside because hey "I am superwoman." I went through four rounds of chemotherapy, having monthly, bi-annual, and now yearly check-ups. There were a couple of other cancer scares along the way that were found to be benign. It had been 20 years, and I was still cancer free! Still trying to be everything for everyone except myself. Basing my decisions on how they will affect others instead of putting myself first.

This brings us back to the question I was asked November 2023, "what do you want". I started doing inner work with an awesome coach, Joanne Barnes, who has shown me how to be honest with myself. For so long I went by the phrases "fake it till you make it" and "never let them see you sweat." I am finally putting my oxygen mask on first. Yes, I am a mom, grandmother, aunt, sister, and friend but I am learning to love me, embrace joy and live for me.

Moms, take time for yourself. Have something that you do just for you. Maybe it's a pedicure, a walk in the park to smell the fresh air and see all the natural beauty God created. Hair appointments are underrated, I take my best naps under the dryer and those scalp massages feel like heaven!

I have a space in my bedroom that I am beautifying, it is called my "peace place." It has my chaise lounge, a lamp and table for my books and journals and my most comfortable blanket. This is my space for meditation, reading and maybe taking a nap lol.

I am learning more everyday about who I am, saying out loud what I like and don't like and embracing saying no without an explanation. I am in love with Dee Dee and she is amazing! I am happy and excited to see what each day holds for me and that I am the creator of those experiences. I choose joy, peace, abundance and remain open to new opportunities daily.

Love yourself and to thine own self be true.

Dionne Anderson

Dionne Anderson was born and raised in Detroit, Michigan and is a graduate of the Detroit Public School system. She attended Western Michigan University and graduated from Detroit College of Business (presently Davenport University) with a bachelor's degree in health administration in 1993.

She has worked for Department of Homeland Security-U.S. Citizenship and Immigration Services for 27 years. She has held several positions during her tenure and presently is a Supervisory Operations Support Specialist.

She is a small business owner representing Mary Kay and uses her business as another avenue to inspire, enrich and make a difference in women's lives. Collaborating by partnering with like-minded individuals

She has one grown son, Trevor, two grandsons; Tyler Harvey and Elijah Dionne Anderson who are the light of her life.

She is a 22-year breast cancer overcomer and truly believes it is a diagnosis not a death sentence.

Her greatest desire is to empower women to see themselves as God sees them and to make a positive impact in the lives of everyone that she encounters. Her favorite scripture is Psalms 139:14 NASB "I will give thanks to You, for I am fearfully and wonderfully made; Wonderful are Your works, and my soul knows it very well."

Contact Information:

Email: dkaspirit@gmail.com
Instagram: @vivacious_dee1

Chapter Ten

Tina Silver

Unshaken: A Mother's Path to Joy Through Trials

"You're not going to be anything." Those words were etched into my soul long before I even knew what they meant. My grandmother's voice carried a conviction that was impossible to escape, and over time, her words became my reality. My mother had signed over her parental rights when I was young, leaving me to be raised by my grandparents. They gave me a roof over my head, but love was something I rarely felt. My grandmother's words weren't just critical—they were cutting. Every mistake I made, every decision that didn't meet her standards, seemed to confirm that I wasn't enough.

By the time I was a teenager, I was desperate for freedom. My grandmother's house wasn't a home—it was a place where I felt small and unseen. When I found out I was pregnant at 18, I thought I had found my way out. My daughter, Faith Divine, was my glimmer of hope, the promise of a new beginning. I thought that becoming a mother would give me the purpose and love I had always searched for. But nothing about motherhood came easy.

"Before there is joy, there is pain." These words are more than a statement; they're a truth that has been lived and felt through generations of my family. People love to speak about joy, about the breakthroughs and the victories, but the road to joy is paved with pain. It's messy, raw, and full of lessons that test your strength in ways you never imagined. Resilience isn't just a nice word—it's a necessity. It's the ability to keep going when everything in you wants to give up.

Joy is often described as a feeling of great pleasure and happiness, but for me, joy is deeper than fleeting emotions. It's the peace that comes after enduring the storm, the calm that follows chaos. It's knowing that despite everything, God is still working, still moving, and still faithful.

Resilience is the ability to bounce back, to withstand hardship and keep moving forward even when you feel broken. It's the refusal to let pain define you or steal your hope. Resilience is a choice, a mindset that says, "This won't break me."

The truth of the matter is that my family has carried the weight of a generational curse for too long. My great-grandmother was an alcoholic, and the pain she caused my grandmother was passed down to my mother. My mother, unable to handle the weight of her own wounds, passed them on to me. And unknowingly, I passed them on to my daughter, Faith. But the curse stops here. It has to stop here. I am determined to kill this generational curse so it does not touch my granddaughter.

Moments for Moms III: Journeys of Joy and Resilience

When I got pregnant with my daughter, I didn't know God deeply I knew Him on a surface level, but I hadn't yet experienced His transformative power. One day, I opened a Bible that I had seen sitting on a friend's table. I began to read about faith, and something stirred in me. I decided to name my daughter Faith, and her father added Divine, giving her the name *Faith Divine*.

After Faith was born, life didn't suddenly become easier. I moved back to my grandmother's house, trying to find my footing. Six months later, I found out I was pregnant with my son, William. Back at my grandmother's house, I was on welfare and enrolled in various programs, doing everything I could to provide for my children. I was determined to create a better life for them, even if I didn't yet know how.

Then I met someone I thought was my Prince Charming. He offered me the promise of stability and love, but it wasn't long before the fairytale turned into a nightmare. He was abusive, and I stayed in that toxic relationship for 10 years. The years of enduring his violence and control took a toll not only on me but on my children, who witnessed far more than they ever should have.

Finally, I found the strength to leave. I moved to North Carolina, filed for divorce, and began the challenging journey of starting over as a single mom. But this time, I was determined to rebuild my life. With God's help, I worked hard to ensure that my children never experienced the kind of trauma I had endured. We didn't live in an apartment—we always lived in a house. I made sure they grew up in safe neighborhoods, surrounded by the kind of stability and security I never had.

I worked tirelessly to provide for them, ensuring they had the best opportunities. On the outside, everything seemed to be going well I had a steady job, and we attended church regularly. I even started a mentorship program for teenage girls, pouring into them the wisdom and love I had learned through my own trials. Life appeared to be coming together, and for a while, it felt like I was finally moving in the right direction.

But then the ball dropped.

When Faith came to me at 16 and told me she was pregnant, my world felt like it was crumbling. I had worked so hard to shield my children from pain, to break the generational curse, and now it seemed like it was all happening again. Faith ran away and moved in with her dad, leaving me heartbroken and questioning everything. Despite all my efforts, she still had to walk her own path, and I couldn't stop it.

This season pushed me to my breaking point. I spiraled into a mental breakdown, overwhelmed by guilt, shame, and feelings of inadequacy. I had done everything I could to give my kids a better life, so why did it feel like I had failed? I questioned my ability as a mother and even my faith in God.

But in that brokenness, God met me. He reminded me that I was never in control to begin with. He showed me that just as He had to purify me through my trials, He was purifying Faith through hers. Tough love is the best love, and sometimes the greatest act of love is stepping back and allowing God to work.

Faith eventually came back home. While I was grateful to have her return, our relationship was never quite the same. There was a distance between us that hasn't fully healed to this day. But I'm learning to trust God's timing, not my own. Writing this and sharing my story has shown me that the generational curse is broken, and I believe that God is restoring our relationship, even if I can't see it yet.

Through this journey, I've come to understand that being a mother is one of the hardest, most beautiful callings. It's not about perfection. It's about doing the best you can, trusting God with what you can't, and giving yourself grace. Looking back, I see now that what I thought was a failure was really God testing my faith—testing my ability to trust Him with my children's lives.

The truth is, motherhood will test your faith. It will push you to your limits and force you to let go of control. But that's where God steps in. My daughter's name is Faith Divine, and I realize now that God was teaching me through her name what this journey is all about: *Faith is the substance of things unseen.* Even when we can't see it, God is working. Even when our children stray, He is guiding them.

In the midst of my pain, I found God. He was there all along, even in the moments when I felt most alone and unworthy. God knew every step of my journey before I even took my first. He knew the challenges I would face, the tears I would cry, and the mistakes I would make. And in His divine wisdom, He had me name my daughter *Faith*.

Faith and Will—my children are a reflection of the journey God was calling me to walk. Through them, He taught me what it means to endure, to persevere, and to trust Him when nothing makes sense. Faith reminded me to believe in what I could not see, and Will reminded me to push forward even when I felt like giving up. They are more than my children; they are the evidence of God's grace in my life.

To every mother reading this, hear me when I say: **you are enough.** No matter what your past looks like, no matter what mistakes you've made, you are a good mother because you showed up, you loved, and you did the best you could.

You don't need a perfect background to be a good mom. You don't need a blueprint. You don't need the approval of others. What you need is God. And when you give Him the broken pieces, He will create something beautiful.

Stop blaming yourself for the choices your children make. Their journeys are not a reflection of your worth as a mother. Just as God allowed you to go through your own process to refine and purify you, He is doing the same for them. Let go of the guilt, the shame, and the weight of trying to control what was never yours to control. **Give it to God, and trust that He will take care of the rest.**

The generational curse stops with you. Your willingness to face your pain, to fight for your children, and to trust God has already broken chains you can't even see. Your obedience is planting seeds that will bear fruit in your children and generations to come.

Powerful truths to hold onto:

- *"For I know the plans I have for you," declares the Lord, "plans to prosper you and not to harm you, plans to give you hope and a future."* (Jeremiah 29:11)

God's plans for your children are greater than anything you can imagine. Trust Him.

- *"Train up a child in the way he should go, and when he is old he will not depart from it."* (Proverbs 22:6)

The seeds you've planted in your children's lives will grow, even if you don't see the harvest yet.

- *"And we know that in all things God works for the good of those who love Him, who have been called according to His purpose."* (Romans 8:28)

Even in your pain, God is working. Even in your mistakes, He is moving.

- *"Come to me, all you who are weary and burdened, and I will give you rest."* (Matthew 11:28)

You don't have to carry this weight alone. Surrender it to God, and let Him give you rest.

To the mother who feels like she's failing:
You are not failing. You are fighting. You are showing up every day, doing the best you can with what you have. And that is enough.

To the mother who feels broken:
Your brokenness is not the end of the story. God is using it to write a testimony that will transform lives, including your own.

To the mother who feels tired:
Rest in God's promises. He has not forgotten you, and He never will.

God's timing is perfect. His love is unconditional. And His grace is sufficient. So take your hands off what you're trying to fix and let Him do what only He can do. Trust Him with your children, your pain, your future, and your heart.

You are stronger than you think, and you are never walking alone. God is with you, and His plans for you and your family are greater than you can imagine.

Hold onto faith. Hold onto willpower. And hold onto the God who holds you.

Let go, let God, and watch Him do the impossible. **All is well.**

Tina Silver

Tina Marie is a remarkable individual who has shown incredible strength and resilience as a domestic violence survivor. She is the author of the critically acclaimed book "The EXIT STRATEGY," which was released on October 8th, 2023. This powerful guide is specifically designed to help women navigate their way out of toxic relationships and find a path towards healing and freedom. She is also the visionary of the Anthology project, "UNBOUND: Breaking free from Domestic Violence," which was released on October 24th, 2024.

Not only is Tina an accomplished author, but she is also a dedicated realtor. With a deep understanding of the importance of safe and secure homes, she goes above and beyond to assist women in finding the perfect living spaces that promote their well-being and provide a fresh start.

In addition to her work as a realtor, Tina is a Transformational and Business Life Coach. Through her coaching services, she empowers individuals to achieve personal and professional growth. With her insightful guidance, clients are able to overcome obstacles, unlock their true potential, and find success in all areas of their lives.

Tina has gained a reputation as a highly sought-after motivational speaker. Her captivating talks are filled with vulnerability and resilience, leaving audiences inspired and motivated to take action. By sharing her own journey of triumph over adversity, she offers a shining example of how hope can transform even the darkest of circumstances into new beginnings filled with hope and promise.

In all aspects of her life and work, Tina Marie embodies strength, compassion, and a genuine desire to make a positive impact. Her dedication to empowering women and providing them with the tools they need to thrive is truly commendable.

Contact Information:

Facebook: Tina Marie
Website: www.crownsrise.com
Email: info@iamtinamarie.com

Chapter Eleven
Juanita N. Woodson

Grace-Filled Growth

James 1:2-4: "Consider it pure joy, my brothers and sisters, whenever you face trials of many kinds, because you know that the testing of your faith produces perseverance

I became a mom fresh out of high school. Pregnant at 17 and a mother at 18, I was thrust into a world that demanded resilience, faith, and strength I wasn't sure I had. Life didn't give me time to prepare—it simply said, "It's time to grow."

One thing I appreciate now that I'm older is how my parents didn't allow me to hand over my responsibilities as a parent to them just because I was a young mom. They guided me, supported me, and held me accountable, teaching me early on that being a parent meant stepping up, no matter how young or unprepared I felt.

As my son and I both grew, I learned how to find joy in challenging and uncertain seasons. I want to share my story, not because it's perfect, but because it's real. My prayer is that it inspires you to trust God's process, even when you can't see what's ahead.

James 1:2-4: "Consider it pure joy, my brothers and sisters, whenever you face trials of many kinds, because you know that the testing of your faith produces perseverance." This verse became one of my lifelines as I learned to embrace the journey and wait on God.

As a teenager, I had big dreams, like most 17-year-olds getting ready to graduate high school, college, a career, and the freedom to chart my own path. But everything changed when I found out I was pregnant at 17. My life was no longer just about me; I had a new purpose, one I wasn't sure I was ready for.

When I was pregnant, I felt more fear and anxiety than joy. My mind raced with questions and doubts. Would my child be healthy? What kind of mother would I be? How would I handle everything? I desperately wanted to protect the life growing inside of me and prayed nothing would go wrong. Yet, I also had no idea what I would do when he finally arrived.

The first time I heard my son's heartbeat, those emotions collided in a way I'll never forget. Fear and uncertainty were still there, but so was a flicker of joy. And with it came an overwhelming sense of purpose that I couldn't ignore. That tiny sound reminded me that God was in control, even when I wasn't.

Becoming a mother at 18 reshaped my entire perspective on life. I learned patience through sleepless nights and tough decisions. I discovered the depth of unconditional love in ways I never imagined. Most importantly, my faith grew stronger as I leaned on God to guide me through the moments where I felt I didn't have the strength to go on. My son didn't just change my life, he gave it new meaning.

When I found out I was pregnant, fear was my first reaction. I couldn't stop thinking about what my future would look like, how I would provide for my child, and whether I was truly ready for this life-changing responsibility. The weight of it all felt crushing at times, and I wasn't sure where to turn.

In the middle of my fear, I turned to prayer. I asked God for clarity, peace, and strength, even when I didn't feel capable of carrying this new role. I leaned on my family, who became my anchor during uncertain times. I had an amazing support system that refused to let me give up, reminding me constantly of the strength I already had within me.

Thankfully, I graduated high school before having my son. But once he arrived, I had to figure out what was next. Could I still go to college? Would I be able to balance being a mother and pursuing an education? These questions loomed over me, but I was determined not to let them stop me.

I turned to prayer, asking God for clarity and strength. My amazing support system, including my family, refused to let me give up, reminding me that I had the drive to make things happen. With their encouragement and my own hard-working spirit, I found a way forward.

I enrolled in online classes, which allowed me to work and care for my son while continuing my education. It wasn't easy, but I knew that building a better future for both of us required sacrifice and perseverance.

The journey was far from smooth. Between the demands of motherhood, working to provide for my son, and keeping up with my classes, there were times when I felt overwhelmed. But every time I questioned whether I could handle it all, God showed up.

Through late-night study sessions, early morning feedings, and long workdays, I leaned on my faith and the people around me. My support system was always there to lift me up, and God provided the strength I needed to push through. Each small victory, whether it was passing a class or getting through a tough day, was a reminder that I was capable of more than I realized.

By staying focused and trusting in God's plan, I was able to lay the foundation for a brighter future—not just for me, but for my son as well.

Joy came in the most unexpected ways, often when I needed it the most. Holding my son for the first time was a moment I'll never forget—the way his tiny hand wrapped around my finger felt like a promise that everything was going to be okay. Then there were the simple, everyday moments that brought so much light to my life: his first smile, the sound of his laughter, and the day he called me "Mommy" for the first time.

Now, seeing him at 17 years old, excelling in school and already embracing an entrepreneurial mindset just like me, fills my heart with pride. Those early days of uncertainty and hard work were worth it because I see the man he is becoming. Watching him chase his dreams is a constant reminder that, despite the challenges, I've done a great job as his mother.

One of the most profound lessons I've learned is that joy isn't about having a perfect life; it's about finding gratitude in the midst of the chaos. It's choosing to see the beauty in the small victories and the blessings hidden in the struggles.

I also learned to trust in God's timing. There were moments when it felt like He was silent, but looking back, I see that He was working things out for my good all along. Joy comes from knowing that even when life doesn't go according to my plan, God's plan is always right on time. Through it all, I've learned to cherish the journey and embrace the joy that comes with trusting Him completely.

Life as a mother has taught me that joy and resilience go hand in hand. Joy isn't about the absence of struggles; it's about finding moments of gratitude and beauty in the midst of them. Resilience is what keeps us moving forward when the challenges feel too heavy to bear, reminding us that with God, we are stronger than we ever imagined.

Finding joy as a mother means cherishing the little moments—your child's laughter, their first steps, or the pride you feel watching them grow. It's about seeing God's goodness in the chaos and celebrating the victories, big or small.

Resilience is the strength to keep going when life feels overwhelming. It's the decision to rise after every setback, to persevere when the path is unclear, and to trust that God is equipping us for every step of the journey.

As mothers, we embody both joy and resilience. We learn to smile through tears, to stand firm in faith, and to embrace the beauty of our journey, even when it's hard. By choosing joy and walking in resilience, we not only transform our lives but also inspire our children to do the same. Let us continue to trust God's plan, celebrate our progress, and find strength in the knowledge that we are never walking this journey alone.

1. Embrace the Small Moments
Take time to appreciate the small, everyday moments with your children. Whether it's a shared laugh, a quiet moment, or a simple conversation, these are the times that will bring you the most joy. Practice gratitude for the little things, and you'll find that joy becomes easier to recognize, even in difficult circumstances.

2. Build a Support System
No mother can do it alone. Surround yourself with people who encourage, uplift, and support you through the ups and downs of motherhood. Whether it's family, friends, or a community of other mothers, having a strong support system can provide the resilience you need to keep going when things get tough.

3. Lean into Your Faith
When challenges arise, remember to lean into your faith. Prayer, reflection, and trusting in God's plan can provide peace, clarity, and the strength to keep moving forward. In moments of doubt or fear, remember that you're never alone—God is with you, guiding you every step of the way.

Juanita N. Woodson

Juanita N. Woodson is a devoted wife, nurturing mother, and an inspiring force in both her personal and professional life. As a best-selling author, she skillfully weaves her testimony into books that captivate and uplift readers around the world.

Juanita is the visionary owner of Grace 4 Purpose Publishing Co. LLC, where she empowers aspiring authors to transform their stories into published works. Through her coaching and guidance, she fosters creativity and equips individuals with the tools to navigate their writing and publishing journeys successfully.

In addition to her publishing endeavors, Juanita is the founder of *The Authors Impact Hub* community, a thriving space designed to connect, support, and inspire writers as they pursue their dreams. She is also one of the co-founders of the *H.O.P.E. Podcast* (*Helping Organize Positive Parenting Effectively*), a platform dedicated to empowering and supporting teen moms and young adults through meaningful conversations and resources.

A multifaceted entrepreneur, mentor, and advocate, Juanita balances her roles with grace and determination. Her passion for empowering others and fostering creativity leaves an indelible mark on the literary and personal development landscapes. Juanita N. Woodson continues to inspire and uplift those around her, building a legacy rooted in resilience, purpose, and faith.

Contact Information:

Email: contact@grace4purposeco.com
Instagram: @_juanitanicole_
Facebook: Juanita Nicole Woodson
Website: www.grace4purposeco.com

Moments for Moms III: Journeys of Joy and Resilience

Join The Moments for Moms Community

 @m4mlegacyunlocked

Check out the Moments for Moms collection

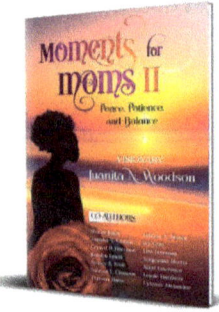

Moments for Moms II: Peace, Patience, and Balance

Moments for Moms: Give Yourself a Minute

Moments for Moms III: Journeys of Joy and Resilience

www.grace4purposeco.com

www.ingramcontent.com/pod-product-compliance
Lightning Source LLC
Chambersburg PA
CBHW072202160426
43197CB00012B/2484